GOING TO THE DENTIST

by Nicole A. Mansfield

raintree

a Capstone company — publishers for children

Raintree is an imprint of Capstone Global Library Limited, a company incorporated in England and Wales having its registered office at 264 Banbury Road, Oxford, OX2 7DY – Registered company number: 6695582

www.raintree.co.uk
myorders@raintree.co.uk

Editorial credits
Editor: Ericka Smith; Designer: Sarah Bennett; Media researcher: Svetlana Zhurkin; Production specialist: Katy LaVigne
Consultant credits: Patricia V. Hermanson, DMD, MS

ISBN 978 1 3982 5046 8 (hardback)
ISBN 978 1 3982 5045 1 (paperback)

British Library Cataloguing in Publication Data
A full catalogue record for this book is available from the British Library.

Acknowledgements
Getty Images: Blend Images–Peathegee Inc., 16, ftwitty, 13; Shutterstock: Andriyana Dadan, cover (design elements), BearFotos, 4, Carolina Soto Ramos, 8, Dariusz Jarzabek, 9, Designifty, 1 (smiling tooth), Desizned, 14, Doro Guzenda, 10, Gatot Adri, 15, Kzenon, 17, Lucky Business, 5, luckyraccoon, 6, Markus Kaemmerer, 7, Nata Kotliar, 11, Peakstock, cover, Perfectorius, cover (design elements), poonsap, 19, Rvector (background), 3, 22, 23, 24, Serhii Bobyk, 18, Zhanna Markina (background), cover, bac[...], Zhurkin: 21

Every effort has been made to contact copyright holders of [...]. Any omissions will be rectified in subsequent printings if no[...]

All the internet addresses (URLs) given in this book were v[...]. However, due to the dynamic nature of the internet, some [...]. sites may have changed or ceased to exist since publicatio[...]. regret any inconvenience this may cause readers, no resp[...] be accepted by either the author or the publisher.

Printed and bound in India.

Contents

Words in **bold** are in the glossary.

Visiting the dentist

A dentist is a doctor for your teeth. Going to the dentist for a check-up helps you look after your teeth! You usually go twice a year.

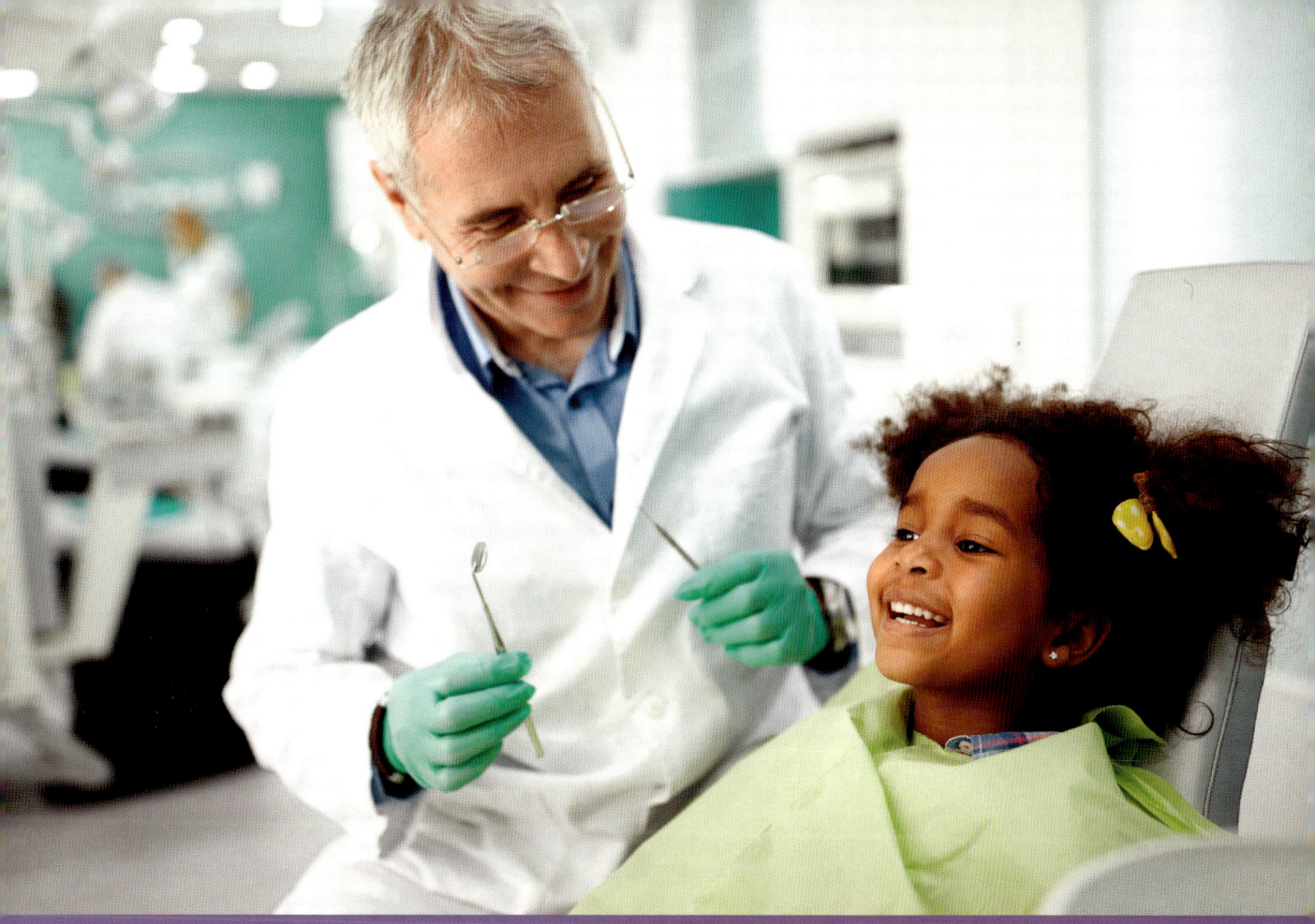

During your check-up, your teeth will be cleaned. They'll also be **inspected**. The dentist will make sure your teeth and gums are healthy.

What to expect

Your check-up will happen in a bright, clean room. The room might remind you of a spaceship!

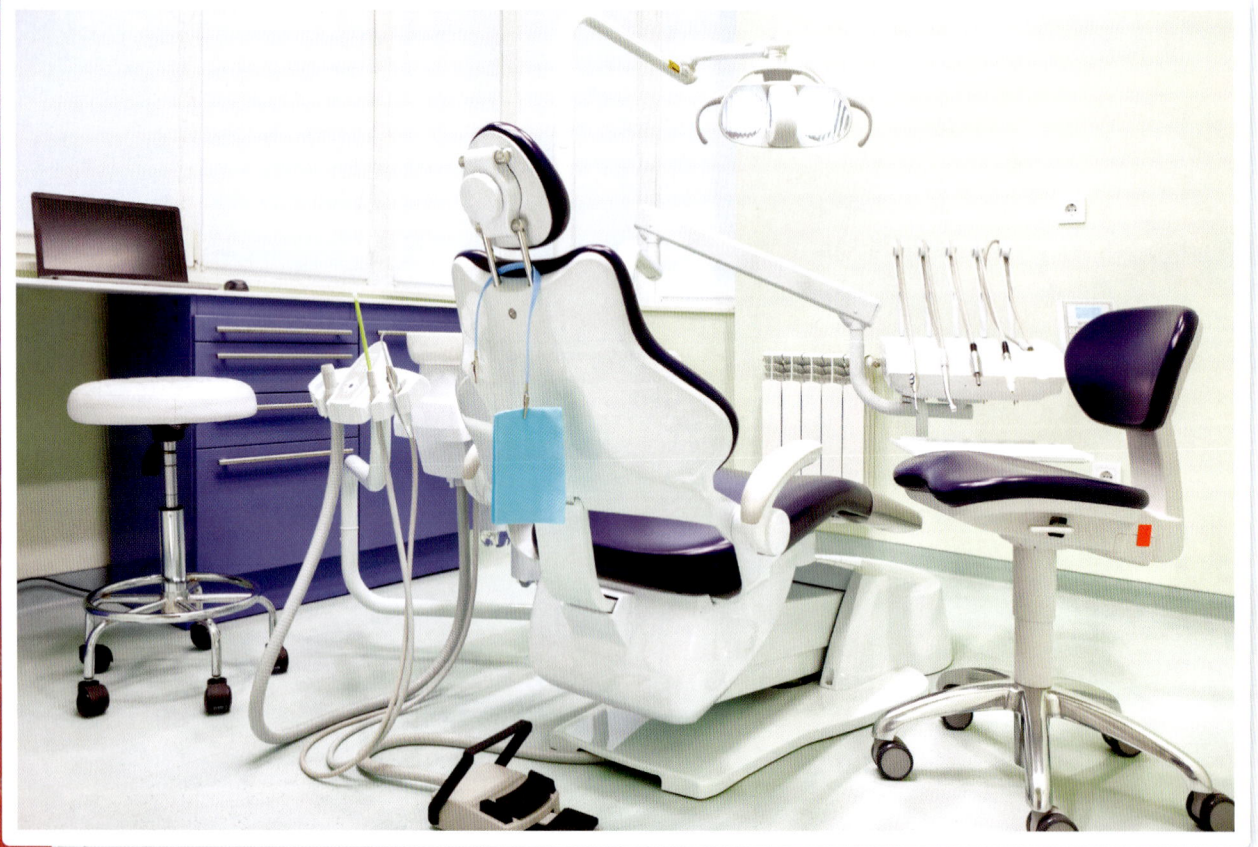

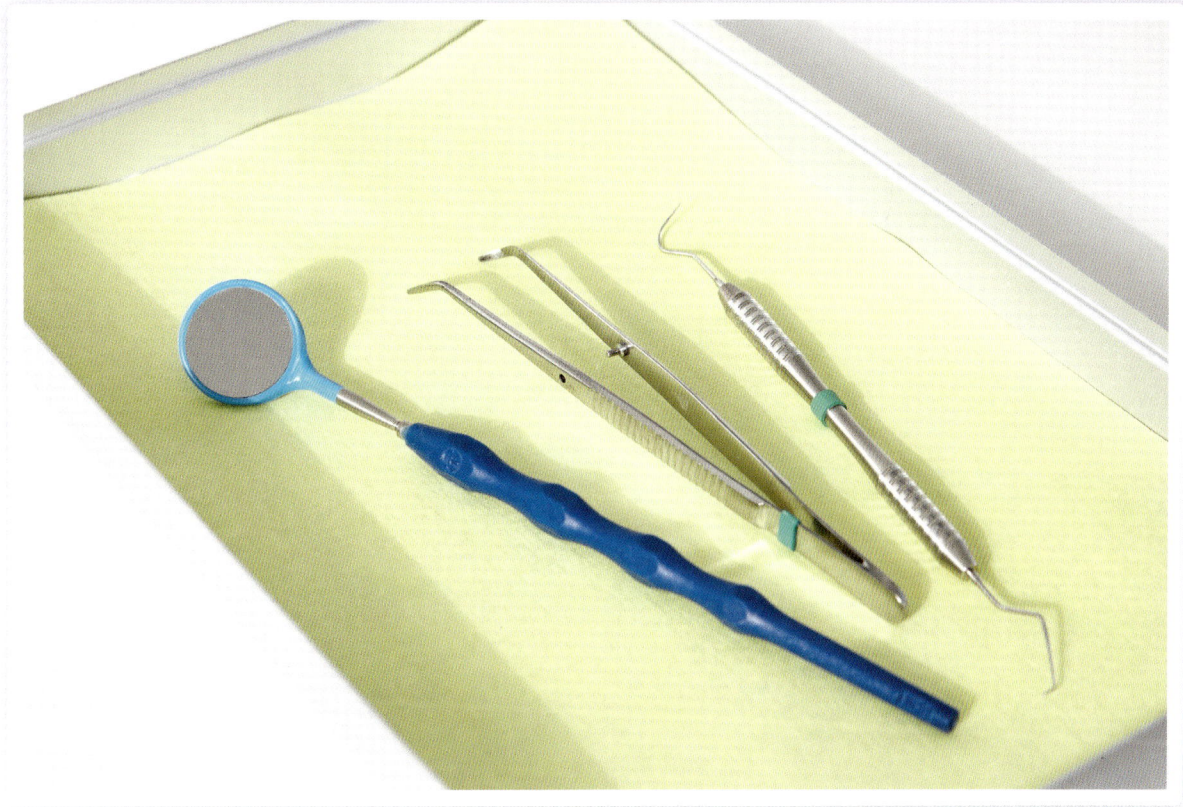

There will be a tray with metal tools on it. One looks like a hook. It helps the dentist to check your teeth. Another has a mirror. It helps the dentist to see inside your mouth.

Some tools may make buzzing noises during your check-up. But don't worry. They won't hurt you!

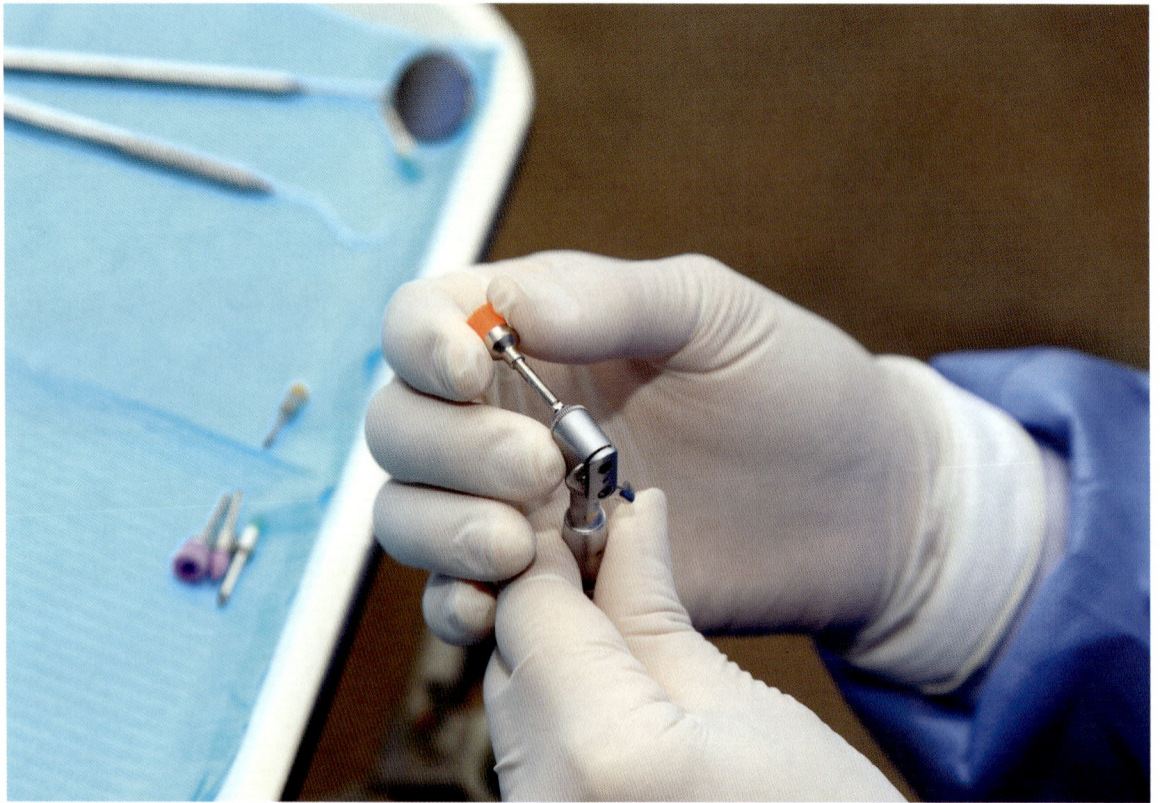

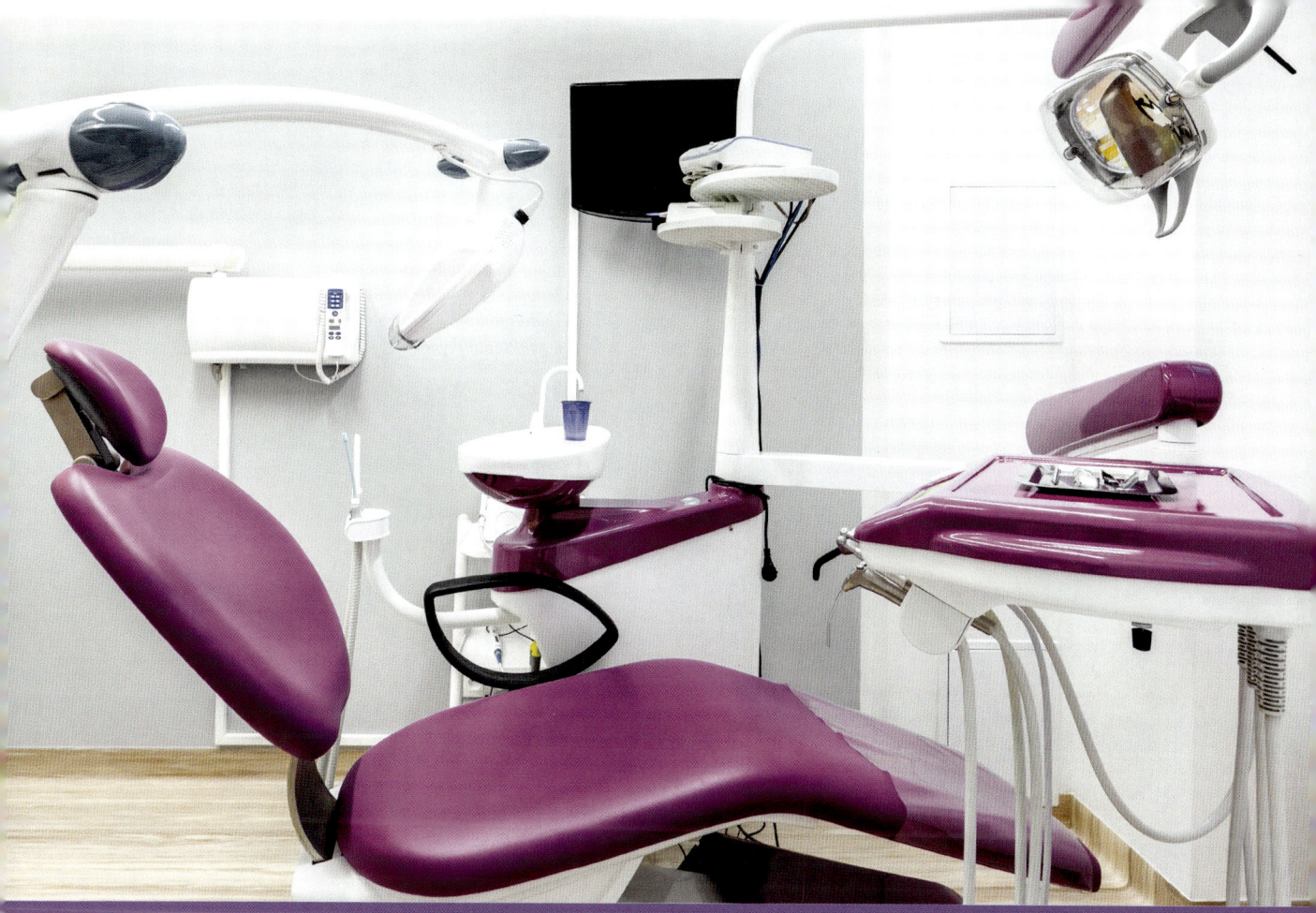

There will be a chair in the middle of the room. The dentist can move it up and down. They can move it back too. This helps the dentist to see inside your mouth.

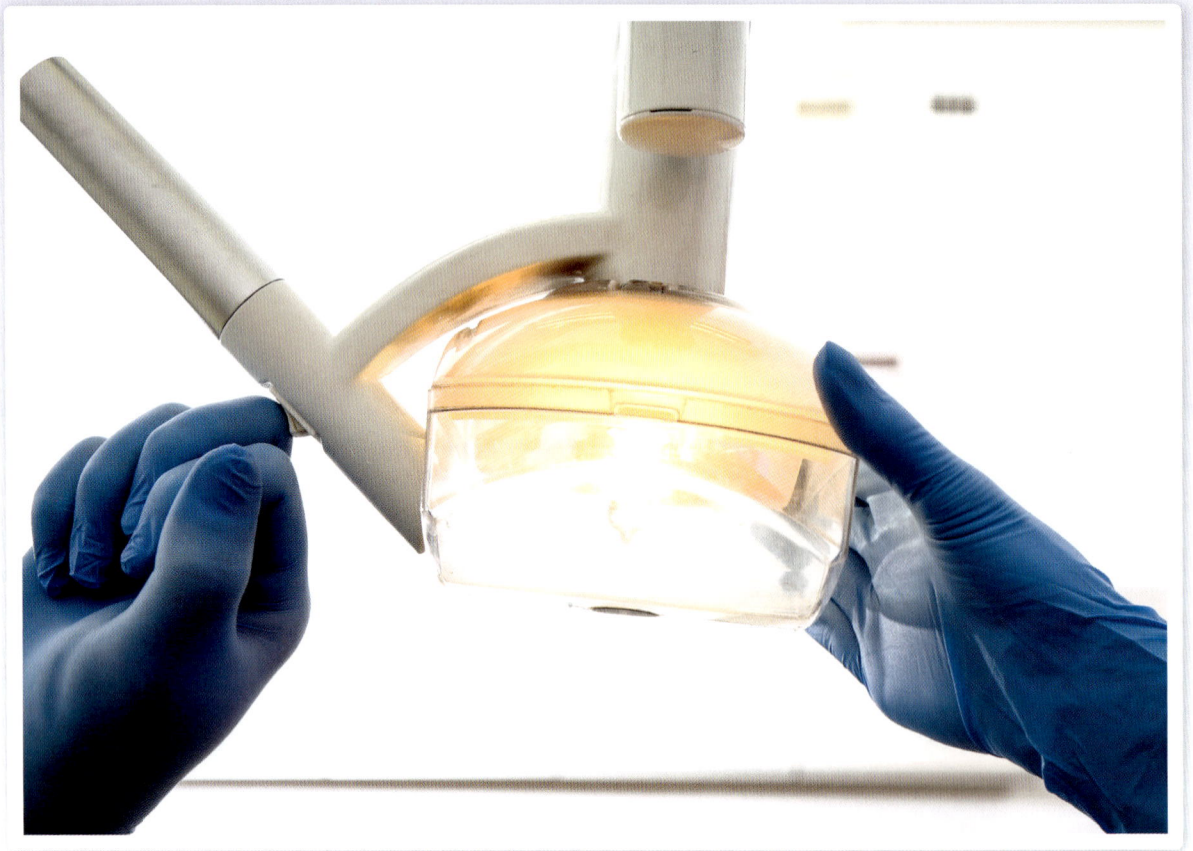

A bright light hangs over the chair.
The light moves too. It helps the dentist
to see your teeth clearly.

You will wear big glasses to **protect** your eyes. You will also wear a bib over your clothes. It will help to keep them clean.

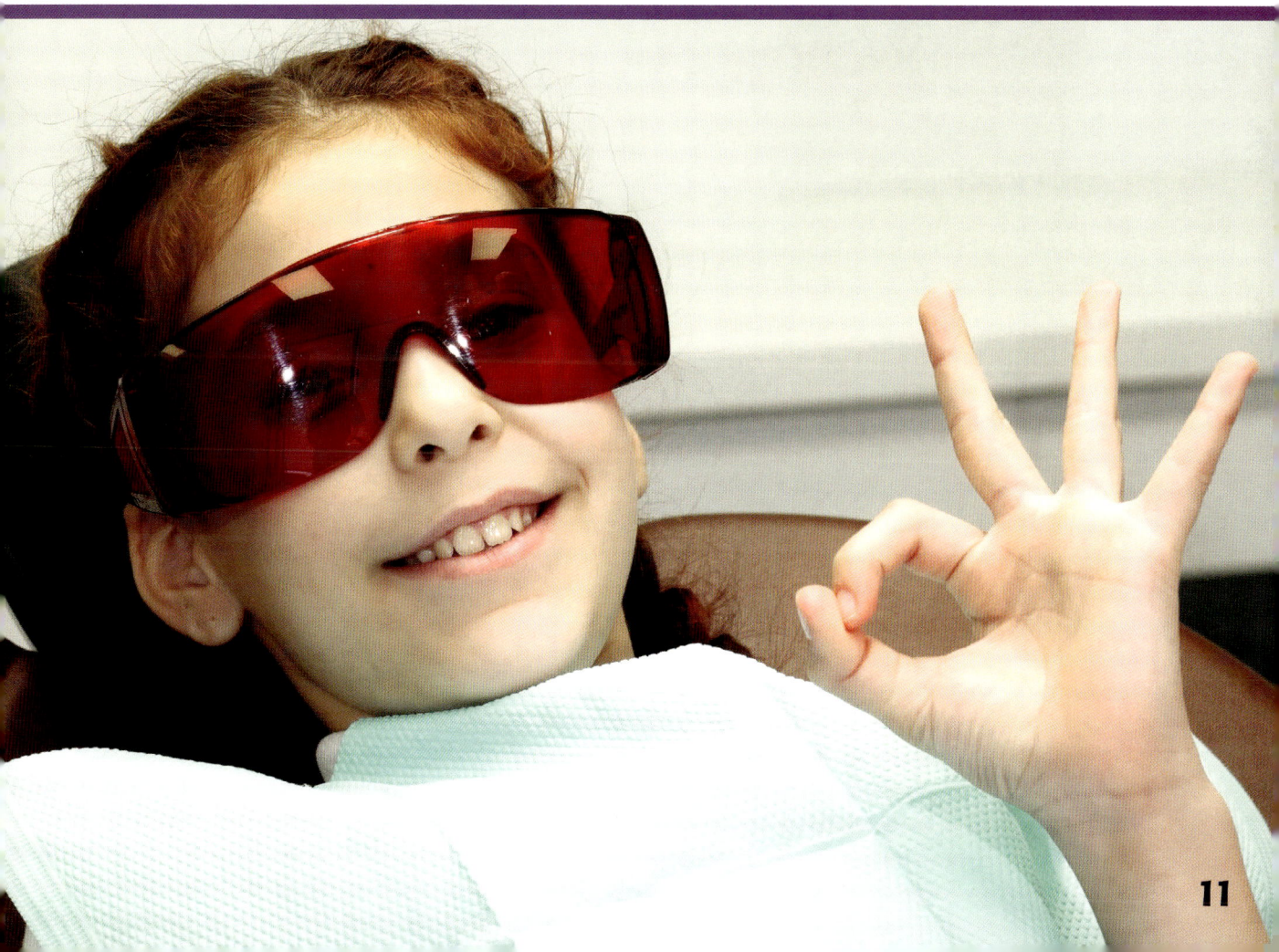

Cleaning your teeth

The dentist's helper will clean your teeth. They use special tools. Their tiny tools can get to places in your mouth that are hard to reach!

After they clean your teeth, they may give you a **fluoride** treatment. Fluoride is a **mineral**. It's like a **vitamin** for your teeth. Fluoride helps to keep them strong!

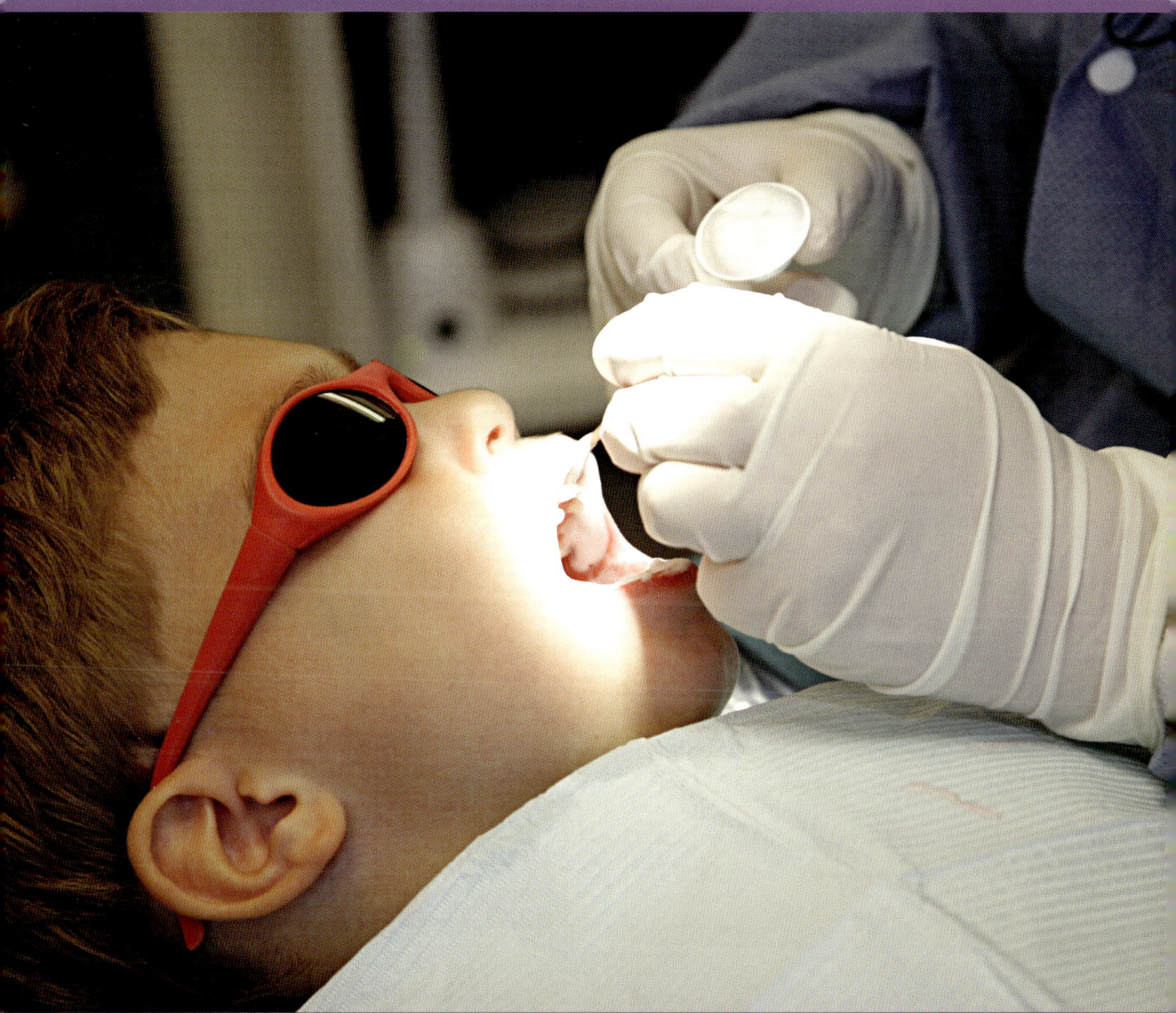

X-rays and more

The dentist or dental nurse might take **X-rays** of your teeth. X-rays show what your teeth look like on the inside. X-rays even show what's below your gums!

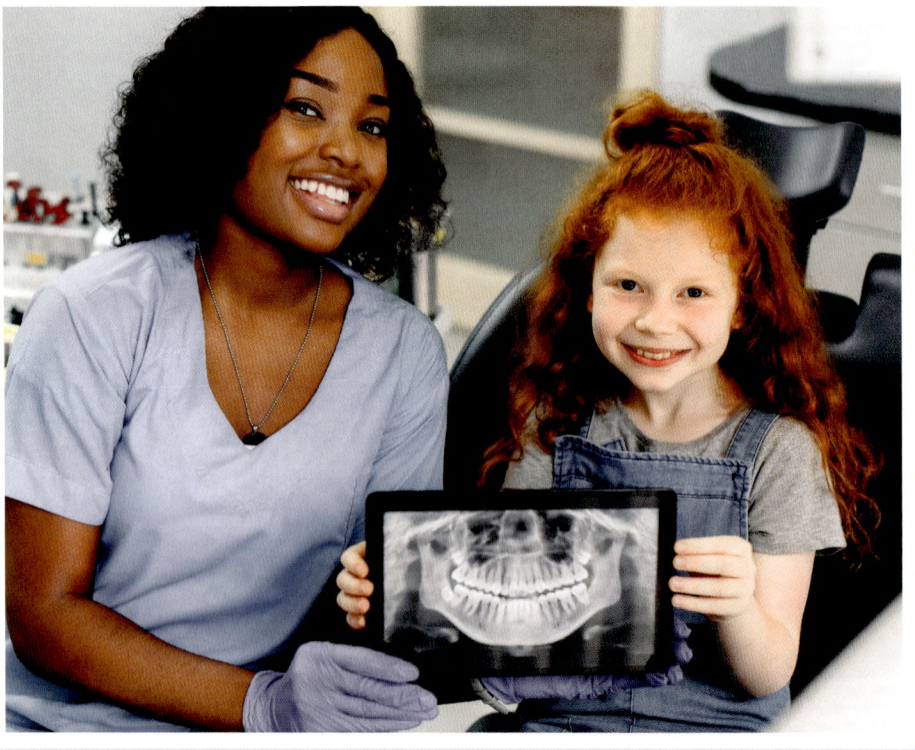

Finally, the dentist will inspect your teeth. They will inspect your gums too. They will look at your X-rays. They might see new teeth below your gums!

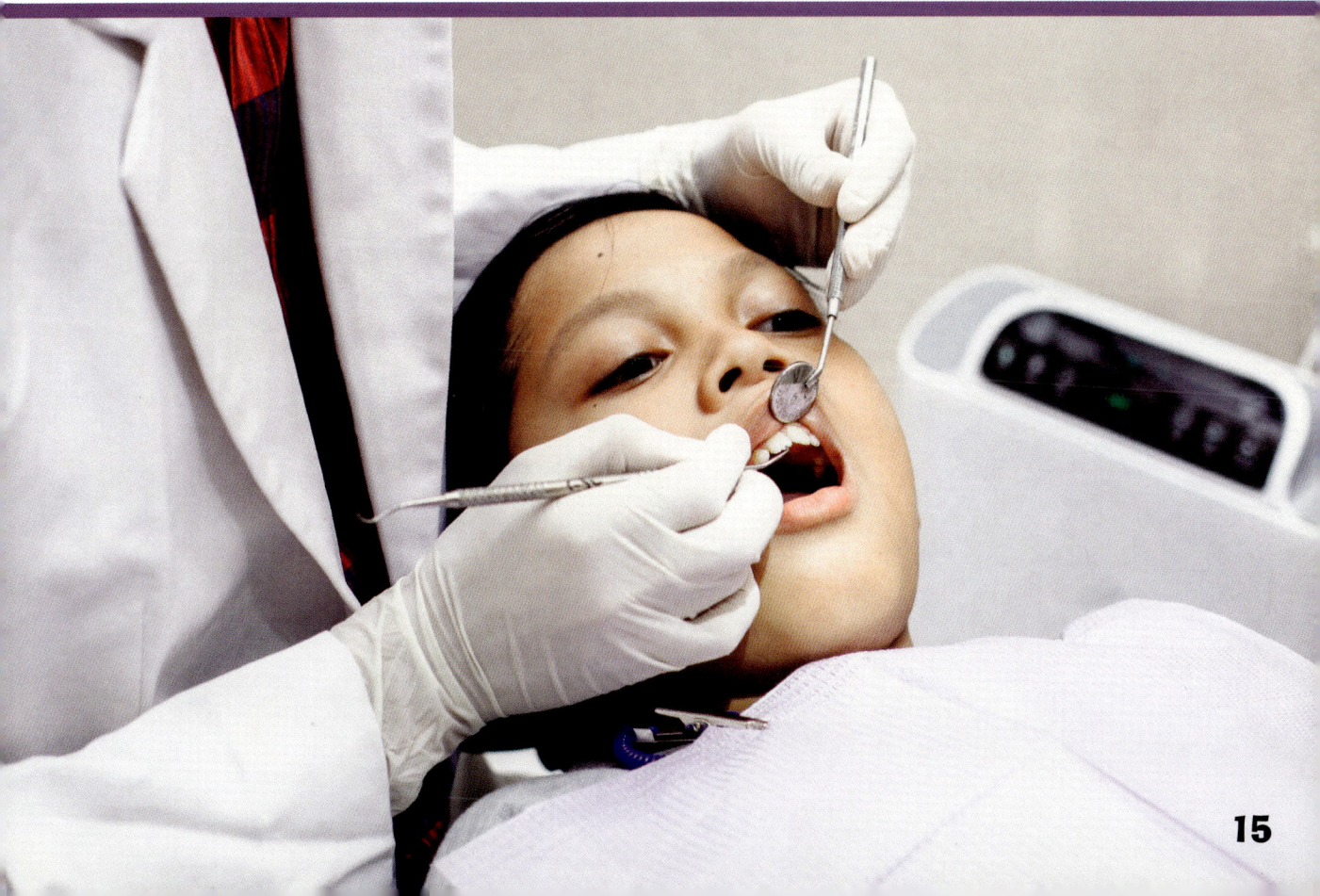

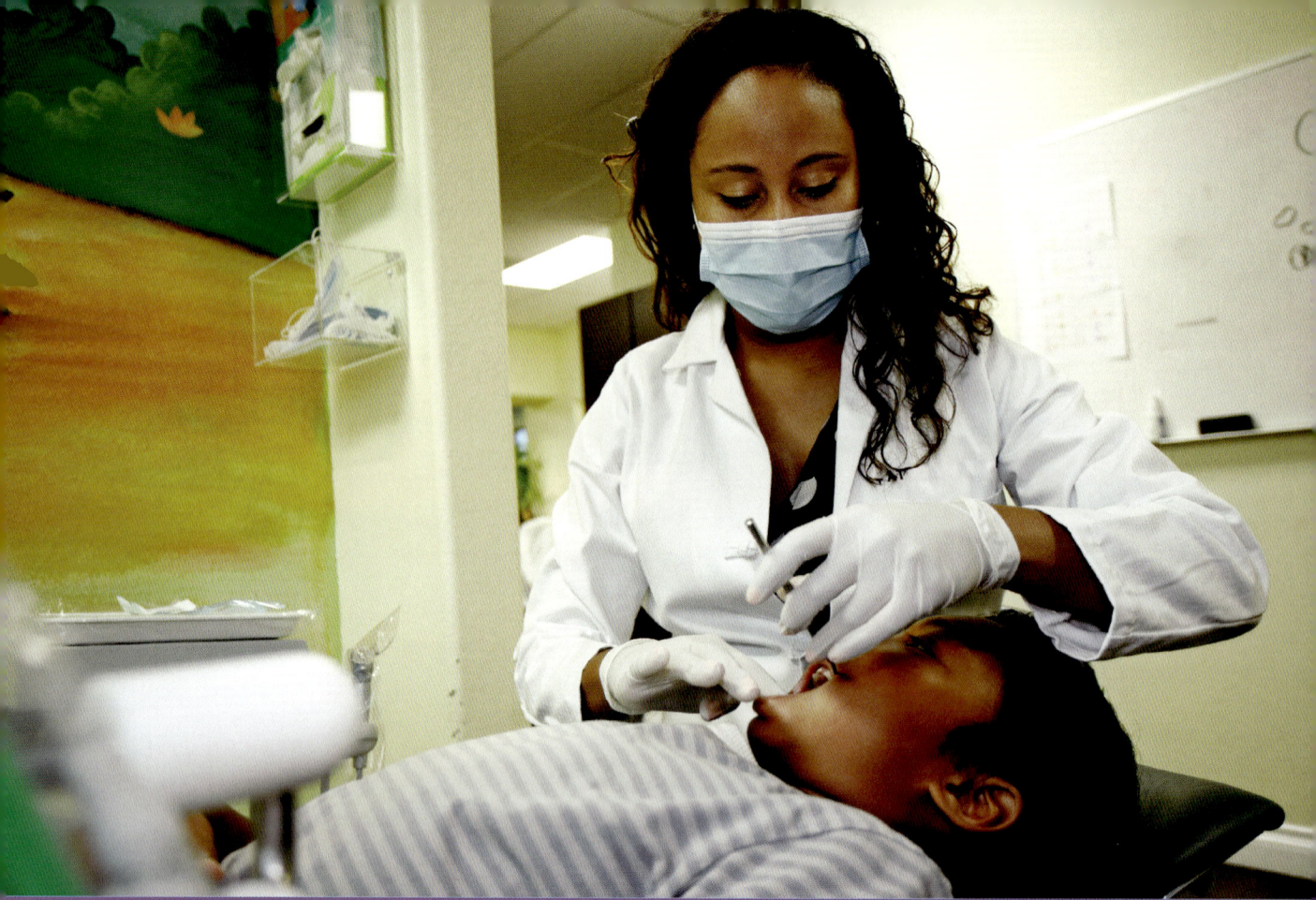

The dentist will check your teeth for **cavities**. A cavity is a hole in your tooth. If you have one, the dentist will fill it. Fillings stop cavities from getting bigger.

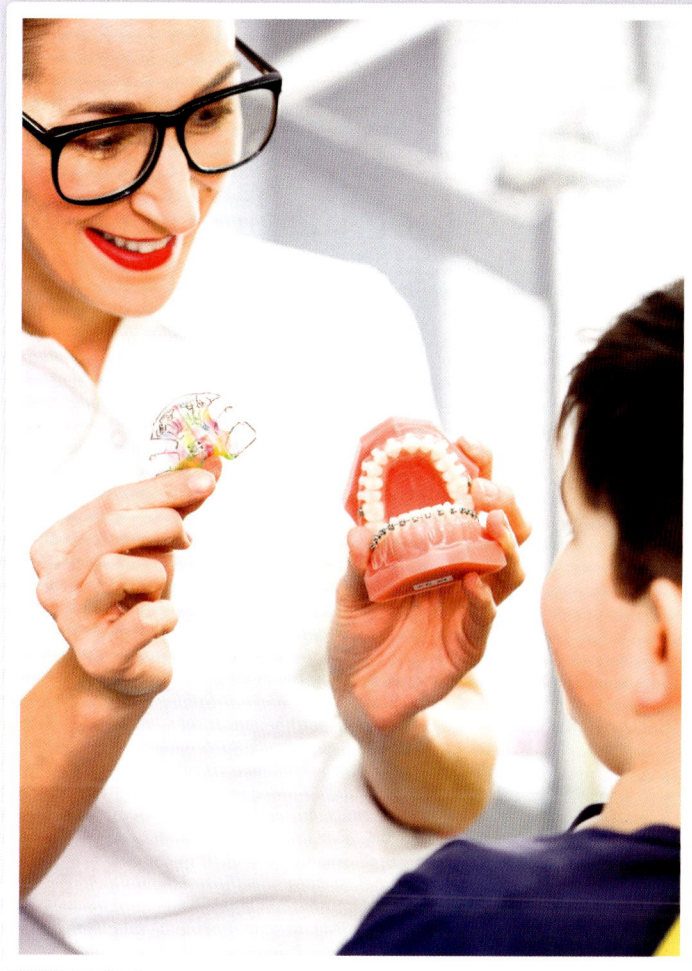

The dentist may also check to see if you will need **braces** in the future. Braces straighten your teeth. Straight teeth do their jobs better.

Keep up the good work!

Dentists and their helpers have important jobs. They know how to clean your teeth. And they know how to fix them.

You have an important job too! Brush your teeth twice a day. And floss once a day. You need your teeth to eat, smile and talk. So take good care of them!

The egg scrubbing experiment

What you need

- 4 hard-boiled eggs
- 4 plastic cups
- 1 cup of vinegar
- 1 cup of regular Cola

- 1 cup of water
- 1 cup of lemonade
- marker pen
- paper

- pencil
- kitchen roll
- 4 toothbrushes
- toothpaste

What you do

DAY 1

1. Put each egg inside a plastic cup.

2. Pour each liquid into a cup. Use the marker pen to label each cup.

3. On your paper, write down what you think each liquid will do to the egg inside the cup.

4. Let the eggs soak overnight.

1. Remove each egg from its cup. Place them all on a sheet or two of kitchen roll.

2. Look at each egg. How did the liquid change the egg? Write on your paper what you see.

3. Use a different toothbrush to scrub each egg. Does scrubbing the egg make it clean? Write the answers on your paper.

4. Add toothpaste to your toothbrushes. Scrub each egg. Does it help to clean the egg better? Write the answers on your paper.

How is this experiment similar to taking care of your teeth? Write down what you have learned.

Glossary

braces metal wires, brackets and bands that are attached to teeth to straighten them

cavity hole in a tooth, caused by decay

fluoride natural mineral that is applied to teeth to make them stronger and help prevent cavities

inspect look at something carefully

mineral material found in nature that is not an animal or a plant

protect cover so that something is not damaged

vitamin substance that helps keep people healthy

X-ray picture of the inside of the body

Find out more

Books

Caring for Your Teeth (Take Care of Yourself), Mari Schuh (Raintree, 2022)

Croc Goes to the Dentist (Experiences Matter), Sue Graves (Franklin Watts, 2022)

Smile! All About Teeth, Ben Hubbard (Raintree, 2019)

Websites

www.bbc.co.uk/bitesize/topics/zcyycdm/articles/z8784xs
Learn more about teeth with BBC Bitesize.

www.youtube.com/watch?v=lQE4xxk1r5g
Dr Ranj gives you tips on how to brush your teeth in this YouTube clip.

Index

About the author

Nicole A. Mansfield dedicates all of her children's books to her own three children – Victorious, Justine and Zion. She lives in Georgia, USA, and is passionate about singing at her church. Nicole loves to go on long walks with her kids and her husband of 19 years.